Emmitt Smith

SPORTS REPORTS

Emmitt Smith

Star Running Back

Jeff Savage

ENSLOW PUBLISHERS, INC.

44 Fadem Road   P.O. Box 38
Box 699   Aldershot
Springfield, N.J. 07081 Hants GU12 6BP
U.S.A.   U.K

Library of Congress Cataloging-in-Publication Data

Savage, Jeff, 1961–
    Emmitt Smith : star running back / Jeff Savage.
       p. cm. — (Sports reports)
    Includes bibliographical references (p.) and index.
    Summary: Describes the life of the man who went from a childhood in a Florida government housing project to become a star for the Dallas Cowboys.
    ISBN 0-89490-653-4
    1. Smith, Emmitt, 1969– —Juvenile literature. 2. Football players—United States—Biography—Juvenile literature. 3. Dallas Cowboys (Football team)—Juvenile literature. [1. Smith, Emmitt, 1969– . 2. Football players. 3. Afro-Americans—Biography.]
    1. Title. II. Series.
    GV939.S635S28 1996
    796.323′092—dc20
    [B]   95-32212
                                              CIP
                                               AC

Printed in the United States of America

10 9 8 7 6 5 4 3 2

Illustration Credits: Courtesy of Dallas Cowboys Weekly, pp. 10, 12, 15, 18, 23, 29, 48, 54, 57, 61, 66, 70, 80, 84, 87, 90, 94; Courtesy University of Florida, pp. 35, 43.

Cover Photo: Courtesy of Dallas Cowboys Weekly

Contents

Chapter 1

A Most Valuable Player

The air was hot and soggy inside the Dallas locker room. Sweat dripped from the players' faces. They were angry and frustrated. It was halftime.

The Cowboys had beaten the Buffalo Bills a year earlier in the Super Bowl by the lopsided score of 52–17. Everyone expected them to crush the Bills again this time. But it wasn't working out that way.

In a Super Bowl rematch, the Bills were leading the 1994 football championship by a touchdown at halftime. The score was 13–6. The Cowboys couldn't believe it. Only six points in a half? How could it be?

Emmitt Smith sat in a corner of the locker room. He was furious. Emmitt had rushed for forty-one yards in the first half. He had caught three passes. It didn't matter. The Cowboys couldn't get in the end zone. The offense had managed just two field goals by Eddie Murray.

The Bills had countered with a pair of field goals by Steve Christie. Buffalo also had the game's only touchdown—a four-yard run by Thurman Thomas.

This was Buffalo's fourth straight trip to the Super Bowl. The Bills hadn't won yet. The Georgia Dome in Atlanta was packed with 72,817 fans. More than 130 million viewers across the country were watching on television. Would the Cowboys lose to the Bills in front of all these people? Not if Emmitt Smith had anything to say about it.

Offensive coordinator Norv Turner approached Emmitt who sat hunched at his locker.

"So," Turner said to Emmitt, "what do you think?"

Emmitt looked up at his coach.

"Get the ball to me," Emmitt said.

"How do you want it?" Turner asked.

"It doesn't matter," Emmitt said. "Just get me the ball."[1]

Four days earlier, Emmitt had been named the Most Valuable Player in the NFL. He had captured his third straight NFL rushing title and led the Cowboys through the playoffs and back to the Super Bowl. None of that mattered now. The season would not be a success unless the Cowboys beat the Bills.

Buffalo returned the second-half kickoff to the twenty-seven yard line and began marching upfield.

Thomas scooted seven yards to the thirty-four. Jim Kelly threw a pass to Bill Brooks to the forty-three for nine more. Emmitt agonized with his teammates on the sideline.

Then the Cowboys made a breakthrough play. Thomas took a handoff up the middle. Defensive lineman Leon Lett reached in and stripped the ball from Thurman's grasp. The ball skidded sideways. Cowboys safety James Washington scooped it up and took off. He zigzagged down the field through the Bills all the way for a touchdown. Eddie Murray kicked the extra point and—POW!—just like that, the game was tied, 13–13.

The Bills couldn't move the ball and had to punt. Dallas took possession at its thirty-six yard line. It was time for the offense to get in gear—time for Emmitt.

Quarterback Troy Aikman called the first play in the huddle. "Power Right," he said.[2] At the snap, Aikman handed the ball to Emmitt. The stocky running back ripped through the Bills' defense for nine yards. Emmitt got the ball again on second down. This time he plowed forward for three yards and a first down.

Aikman called for "Power Right" again. Emmitt took the handoff. Left guard Nate Newton pulled to the right. Fullback Daryl Johnston led Emmitt through the hole. Bills lineman Jeff Wright grabbed

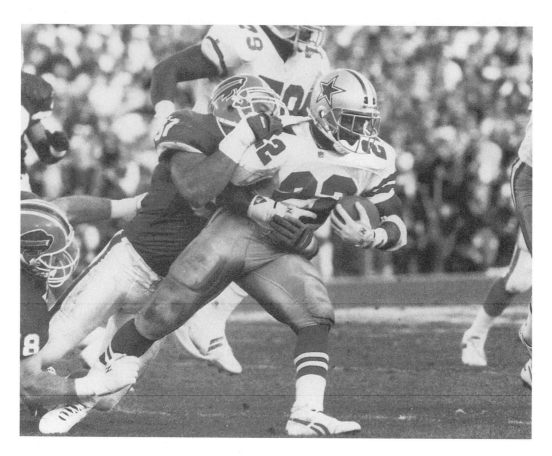

Emmitt charges through the Bills' defense.

Emmitt at midfield. Emmitt carried the 290-pound nose guard four more yards to the Buffalo forty-six for a gain of nine. "Oh my!" television announcer Dick Enberg shouted. "Emmitt Smith looks like a different back in the second half!"[3]

Emmitt got the ball again. He broke lineman Bruce Smith's tackle in the backfield and scampered through the middle for seven yards. The Cowboys were driving. And it was all on the strength of Emmitt Smith.

"Power Right," Aikman said in the huddle. Emmitt took the handoff, powered through Wright, shed the tackle of linebacker Cornelius Bennett, and rumbled down the right sideline where he was tackled by linebacker Darryl Talley at the Bills' twenty-three, a gain of fourteen yards.

Then Power Right again. Emmitt banged ahead five more yards. He lifted himself off the artificial turf and trudged to the Cowboys' sideline. "I need a break," he told Coach Turner. "How many plays?" the offensive coordinator asked. "I need two," Emmitt said.[4]

He got one. Aikman threw a three-yard pass to Johnston, the fullback. Then Emmitt ran back onto the field. He had to finish what he started.

"Power Right," Aikman said in the huddle. The Bills were expecting it. Still they could not stop it.

Troy Aikman is the star quarterback of the Dallas Cowboys. At UCLA, he led the Bruins to a Cotton Bowl victory in 1989.

Jeff Wright shot into the Cowboys' backfield to grab Emmitt just as he took the handoff. Emmitt shook free of Wright's grasp. "Emmitt breaks a tackle!" Enberg shouted on TV. "Ten . . . five . . . Touchdown!"[5] Emmitt burst in for the score!

The Cowboys mobbed Emmitt in the end zone. Offensive tackles Erik Williams and Mark Tuinei hugged him. Receiver Michael Irvin and tight end Jay Novacek slapped him on the helmet. Troy Aikman shook his hand.

The Cowboys led, 20–13.

Buffalo didn't quit. Jim Kelly moved the Bills with passes to Andre Reed and Don Beebe, and soon the Bills reached midfield. But then Kelly underthrew Beebe. James Washington intercepted and returned the ball to the Buffalo thirty-four.

Emmitt took over again. First, he plowed over defensive end Oliver Barnett for six yards. Then, after a Dallas holding penalty, he took a swing pass from Aikman to the right, cut back inside, and broke two tackles to the twenty-five. On third down, he bowled through the line for six more yards and a first down. "We're not talking about a big, bruising kid," TV commentator Bob Trumpy announced. "We're talking about just solid rock inside that uniform!"[6]

The Cowboys fooled Buffalo on the next play.

FACT

Emmitt became the fourth player in NFL history to win three straight rushing titles. The other three were Jim Brown, Steve Van Buren, and Earl Campbell. Brown won five titles in a row.

With everyone expecting Emmitt to get the ball again, Aikman faked a handoff and rifled a pass to Alvin Harper who was tackled at the five.

Now it was up to Emmitt to finish matters. A touchdown would put the Cowboys comfortably in front. On first down, Emmitt smacked ahead for a tough yard. On second down, he banged forward for three more. On third down, he lunged for the goal line, but was stopped inches short.

It was fourth down with ten minutes left. What would coach Jimmy Johnson do? A field goal would give the Cowboys a ten-point lead. Coach Johnson wanted more. He had faith in Emmitt. "I believe in you," the coach said out loud to Emmitt, "and you're going to put it in the end zone."[7]

The Bills looked for Power Right. The Cowboys crossed them up. Aikman pitched the ball back to Emmitt who darted left and skipped across the goal line for the score.

Murray kicked the extra point to make it 27–13. He added a field goal with three minutes left for the final points of the game.

Dallas 30, Buffalo 13.

The Cowboys had scored twenty-four unanswered points in the second half. Emmitt was the hero of the game. He was swarmed by reporters at his locker afterward.

Super Bowl XXVIII MVP Emmitt Smith proudly lifts the Dallas Cowboys' Vince Lombardi Trophy.

"That drive hit them right in the gut," Emmitt said. "It put that doubt in them. They knew they were in trouble."[8]

All around him, the Cowboys shouted with joy. Players took turns hoisting the Vince Lombardi Trophy. Then it was announced: Emmitt had been named Super Bowl MVP.

"Being the MVP of the league and this game, too. You can't ask for anything more," Emmitt said. "It's just been a great, great season for the team and for me."[9]

Chapter 2

Young Running Back

It was a Saturday. The day was cool and overcast. It was a perfect day for football.

The trouble was Emmitt Smith was told not to get dirty. How can you play football and not get dirty?

Emmitt lived in a government housing project in Pensacola, Florida, with his mother Mary, father Emmitt, older sister Marsha, and younger brothers Erik, Emory, and Emil. Emmitt's father drove a city bus and his mother stayed home to take care of the children.

Emmitt had been coming home filthy on weekends so often that his mother threatened him with a whipping if he did it again. But Emmitt loved playing football with his brother Erik and his older cousins. He just *had* to play.

The boys carried their football to a nearby lot. The lot was filled with mud puddles—a great football field! But how were they supposed to keep from getting muddy?

Emmitt thought of a brilliant idea. They could turn their clothes inside out. The boys took off their pants and shirts and put them on inside out. Then they played football.

Before Emmitt and Erik returned home they reversed their clothes again. Now the mud was underneath their pants and shirts. Their mother didn't notice a thing. The trick worked.

A few days later, Emmitt's mother did the laundry. She saw the mud on the clothes. She knew who came up with the idea to fool her—Emmitt. "He got smart," she thought to herself, chuckling.[1]

Emmitt's mother didn't say a word.

There were dangers around the projects. Emmitt sometimes heard shootings at night. Drug dealers roamed the streets. One time, Emmitt and a friend were on their way to football practice when a man in a car pulled up to the curb and called them over. Emmitt thought the man needed directions. He walked over.

"Kid, can you shoot me up?" the man said.

Emmitt didn't understand. "What?" he asked.

"Shoot me up."[2]

The man showed Emmitt a hypodermic needle. Emmitt stared at it a moment, then looked at the

Now that Emmitt makes more than $3 million a year, coming home covered in mud isn't such a bad thing.

man's eyes. They were glazed over. Emmitt and his friend turned and ran as fast they could.

It might have been that incident, or it might have been the solid love and discipline Emmitt received from his parents that kept him from messing with drugs. Emmitt never even experimented with them. He just had no use for them.

When Emmitt was eight, his father built a house in the backyard behind Emmitt's grandparents' house. It was on North G Street, only four blocks from the projects. So even though Emmitt moved away from his neighborhood friends, he could see them anytime.

What Emmitt liked most about his new house was being close to his grandmother. Her name was Erma, but the family called her "Mama." She was a paraplegic.

"Here she was, confined to a wheelchair as long as I knew her," Emmitt says now, "and she never complained once about her life. Never said anything negative. She wasn't able to use her hands, but that didn't stop her from using her mind."[3]

Emmitt's grandfather worked the night shift at a wallboard manufacturing plant. Emmitt was often left to take care of his grandmother. He would fix her dinner as she recited recipes from her wheelchair. Then he would feed her. He would help her

FACT

Emmitt Smith followed five special rules as a child. He says these rules helped make him a superstar in the NFL. Here are Emmitt's five rules:
1. Respect other people.
2. Respect your elders.
3. Go out and put a full effort into your job.
4. Go to school and learn something.
5. Don't go to school to play.[5]

Escambia High football coach Dwight Thomas says we all should follow Emmitt's advice. "Emmitt," coach Thomas says, "is a role model. Not just for kids. I mean for all of us."[6]

into her nightgown and sometimes brush her hair. She would give him advice.

"When I look back over what I did for her," Emmitt says now, "as a kid you don't realize how important what you're doing is. You're saying, 'Darn, I got to do this,' or 'Darn, I got to do that.' Looking back on it now, I'm so happy that I had that opportunity. That taught me about work ethic. It made me responsible, and it taught me to look after other people besides myself, especially when they can't do for themselves."[4]

Emmitt was eight when he joined organized football for the first time. He played for the Salvation Army his first year. Because he was bigger than most kids and seemed more mature, the coach put him at quarterback. Emmitt loved it. He would drop back to pass, look downfield for a second, then, most often, tuck the ball under his arm and take off running.

The following year, Emmitt moved up from Mini-Mites to Mites. On the first day of practice, his coach had a surprise for him. Emmitt was being switched from quarterback to running back. It was crushing news.

Emmitt spent the rest of the week practicing from the tailback position. He took handoffs up the middle and pitchouts around left and right end. He began to enjoy playing tailback. Before long, he fell in love with it.

Emmitt worked on techniques even when he wasn't at practice. To develop balance, he walked on curbs and neighborhood fences. For the next four years, he played tailback in Pop Warner leagues. He developed a reputation around town as a tough-nosed runner, able to dash and dart, but willing to take a hit.

Emmitt was an eighth-grader at Brownsville Middle School when Dwight Thomas became the football coach at Escambia High School. Emmitt would be attending Escambia High in the fall. He wondered about Coach Thomas.

Thomas had coached the previous four years at a bigger Florida high school fifty miles away. The football team compiled a 30–12 record during that time. But the principal demanded a state championship. Coach Thomas was fired.

The only coaching job open for Thomas was Escambia High. The football team hadn't had a winning season in eighteen years. Coach Thomas took the job and immediately went to work. His first task was to visit the middle schools to recruit players for the fall season.

One stop Coach Thomas made was at the Brownsville Middle School.

"All these kids were running around playing run-and-grab-butt, fooling around, normal eighth-grade kids," Coach Thomas remembers. 'Wiggle-worms,' I call them. In the middle of it all there was this quiet kid. He was dressed real nice. Nice polo shirt. Nice pressed slacks. Nice dress shoes. He came over to me and put out his hand. 'Hello, Coach,' he said. 'I'm Emmitt.'"[7]

Escambia High was 1–9 the season before Emmitt arrived. The players were used to goofing off. Football wasn't taken seriously. When Emmitt showed up as a freshman the first day of practice, he learned that twenty-six seniors had been cut. They weren't attending class, so Coach Thomas didn't let them play football.

The football players had three rules: Be where you're supposed to be; be there when you're supposed to be there; and be doing what you're supposed to be doing. Emmitt followed the three rules carefully.

"In Emmitt's four years," Coach Thomas said, "he never missed a practice, never was late for a meeting, and I never heard him say a swear word."[8]

Practice began each day in a classroom where Coach Thomas would deliver a message or discuss a problem. To start the meeting, the coach would flick the light switch to calm everyone down. Every

Emmitt warms up for a Dallas Cowboys practice. Ever since childhood, Emmitt has shown the commitment necessary to be a star football player. As a young man, he never missed a practice.

time the coach flicked the light switch, Emmitt would be sitting in the front row, with a football under his arm, ready to listen.

Coach Thomas had never started a ninth-grader in his coaching career. At Escambia, he started Emmitt at tailback, another freshman, and eleven sophomores.

Escambia won its first game against Pensacola Catholic as Emmitt rushed for 115 yards and scored 2 touchdowns. A high school tailback was born.

The following week against Gulf Breeze High, Emmitt was an open-field wonder, dipping and scooting, making people miss. He ran for 205 yards before being replaced early in the fourth quarter.

Word quickly spread about the marvel at Escambia High. People began showing up at Gators games. Among the crowd was Emmitt's family. In fact, most of the weekend for the Smiths involved football. Saturday mornings, the family watched Erik play Pop Warner football. Saturday nights, they watched Emmitt's father play wide receiver and free safety for the semipro Pensacola Wings of the Dixie League.

Emmitt continued to run through defenses— falling short of the 100-yard mark just twice in 10 games. Once was against rival Pensacola High. Emmitt gained eighty-seven yards, but the Gators were routed, 51–0. They would not forget that embarrassment.

Emmitt rushed for 164 yards against Crestview, 183 against Tallahassee Rickards, 189 against Pensacola Pine Forest, and 210 against Niceville High. The Gators finished with a 7–3 record. They weren't a laughingstock anymore.

After football season ended, Emmitt tried out for the basketball team. He enjoyed the sport and had always been good at it. But he had lifted weights all through football season and ruined his jump shot. At five feet eight inches, he had to play guard. Emmitt made the varsity team, but without an outside shot, he knew he would spend most of his time on the bench. So he quit the team. He tried again as a sophomore, but it was no use. Emmitt decided to focus entirely on football.

Emmitt's sophomore season was a great success. He learned to pick his holes, follow his blockers, and head for the end zone. He ran for 190 yards against Pensacola Pine Forest, 197 yards against Gonzalez Tate, 215 against Niceville, and 218 against Milton.

His best game, though, came against Rickards High. With two sprained ankles, Emmitt thought he'd miss the game. He wasn't even able to run during the pregame warm-ups. He was forced to watch from the sideline as teammate Gerald Williams replaced him at tailback.

Rickards held a touchdown lead late in the fourth quarter when Emmitt pleaded with the coaches to put him in the game. They finally agreed. They taped his ankles tight and sent him in with the offense. Escambia took possession at its own eleven yard line. Emmitt pounded the ball play after play into the Rickards defense. He gained eighty-five yards on the drive and scored the tying touchdown. Escambia won the game in triple overtime. The victory propelled the team into the state playoffs.

The Gators started with a win over Jacksonville Lee. Emmitt had been held to 110 yards rushing, and Coach Thomas decided that if the Gators were to advance to the 3-A semifinals, Emmitt would have to get more yardage. He did just that. The following week against Bartow High, Emmitt slashed and sprinted for 227 yards. In the state championship game, he rushed for 200 in a victory over St. Petersburg Senior.

Emmitt's junior year was even bigger. Escambia had moved up to the 4-A division, the highest level for Florida high schools. The 4-A football champion was considered the best team in the state. The competition would be that much tougher. The Gators found it out right away.

The opening game was against Pensacola Woodham High. Woodham had won the state 4-A title the previous year. To make matters worse, the game was at Woodham. The home team knew what it had to do to win. It had to stop Emmitt. It couldn't.

Emmitt took a pounding in the game. By the second half, his whole body ached. His hip was especially sore after one ferocious tackle. Still, Emmitt rushed for 236 yards. On his last carry, he got drilled by a helmet in his hip again. He could barely walk and had to be helped off the field. The Gators trailed by a point, and the offense stalled. Alan Ward was sent in by Coach Thomas to try a fifty-yard field goal. The kick sailed high and true. Escambia won the game, and Emmitt was the hero.

The entire season went that way for Emmitt. His lowest output of the year was 127 yards against Niceville High. He had seven 200-yard games. And against Milton High, he carried 28 times for 301 yards. On one touchdown run he broke seven tackles. The Escambia running sensation became known throughout the state. One team even took to the field with the number "24"—Emmitt's number—taped to their helmets as a reminder.

Emmitt's running style was beautiful to watch. He had a wiggle in his step to make people miss. He could cut sharply either way without slowing down.

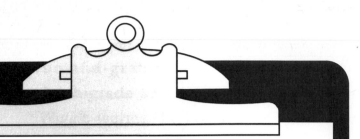

STATS

Emmitt has broken the 100-yard mark more than one hundred times. Here's a list of Emmitt's 200-yard high school games.

YEAR	OPPONENT	YARDS
1983	Pensacola Catholic	205
	Niceville	210
1984	Crestview	236
	Milton	218
	Niceville	215
	Bartow	227
	St. Petersburg Senior	200
1985	Pensacola Woodham	236
	Pensacola Washington	223
	Milton	301
	Pensacola	251
	Pensacola Pine Foest	258
	Tallahasse Leon	277
	Ocala Forest	226
	Auburndale	264
1986	Gonzalez Tate	258
	Niceville	253
	Cardinal Newman	234

Escambia rolled through the season with just one loss to qualify for the 4-A state playoffs. In the first round against Tallahassee Leon, Emmitt rushed for 277 yards. In the quarterfinals against Ocala Forest, Emmitt carried for 226 yards. In the semi-finals against Auburndale, Emmitt ripped for 264 yards.

The state championship game was next. The Gators traveled 400 miles to Lakeland to face mighty Bradenton Southeast High. While Escambia reached the title game largely because of its offense, Bradenton was led by a defense that ranked first in

San Francisco lineman Dennis Brown reaches out for Smith. Taking so many bone-crunching tackles can shorten a running back's career.

the state. But Bradenton proved no match for the Gators. Emmitt rushed for 159 yards as Escambia won by 3 touchdowns.

The 3-A state title. Then the 4-A state title. How could Emmitt's senior year be any better?

It started out that way. Before the season even began, Escambia High was ranked No. 1 in the national polls. Major magazines and TV crews came to Pensacola to do stories on Emmitt and the team.

Emmitt rushed for 170, 171, 169, and 130 yards in the first four games. Then he exploded for 258 and 253 in the next two. The Gators were 6–0, and Emmitt was having fun.

"Sometimes I'd tell the fullback where the hole was going to be before the snap, and the majority of the time I was right," he said. "And sometimes I'd mess around and run to the hole with my eyes closed. Other times I'd take the handoff with just one hand."[9]

Emmitt was toying with opponents. His short bursts of speed were breathtaking. His cutbacks were dazzling. But his best attribute was his *vision*. Emmitt could see the field clearly. He was just a blur to opponents.

Escambia won its next two games to set up a showdown with crosstown rival Pensacola High. Ten thousand people filled Pensacola's stadium,

FACT

Emmitt's favorite team growing up was the Dallas Cowboys, and his favorite player was running back Tony Dorsett.

Emmitt passed the 1,000-yard mark in his seventh game in college—faster than anyone in the history of college football. Emmitt didn't even know about the record until somebody told him after the game.

and five thousand more were turned away at the entrance. The Gators were still ranked first in the nation—but not for long.

The Pensacola defense played tight at the line of scrimmage to try and stop Emmitt. The Gators crossed them up. Wide receiver Marzette Porterfield, a state sprint champion in track, ran a fly pattern and quarterback John Brady threw a perfect pass. Porterfield caught the ball in stride and scored on a sixty-yard bomb. Escambia led, 7–0. After the teams traded field goals, Emmitt broke loose in the third quarter on a fifty-one-yard run down the right sideline for a score. But the officials said he stepped out of bounds. The touchdown was called back, and Pensacola went on to win the game, 17–10.

Escambia won its final two games to finish with a 9–1 regular season record, just as it had the previous year. But for some reason, the Gators did not receive a playoff berth. Emmitt Smith's high school career was over.

It was a difficult ending to a stirring four years for Emmitt. He gained 8,804 yards to move past Billy Sims into second place on the high school all-time rushing list. He scored 103 touchdowns. He gained more than 100 yards in 45 of the 49 games he played in. And through all that, he fumbled just six times. And most important of all, with Emmitt at tailback, Escambia High, long the laughingstock of the Florida Panhandle, amassed a record of 42–7.

"For four years we did three things, and won two state championships doing them," Coach Thomas said. "Hand the ball to Emmitt, pitch the ball to Emmitt, throw the ball to Emmitt. Everyone knew we were going to get the ball to him. It was just a question of how."[10]

Chapter 3

Gators

The first letters began arriving while Emmitt was a sophomore. By his junior year, they were pouring in. It seemed that every college in the country wanted Emmitt Smith.

It was no wonder. *USA Today* and *Parade* magazine named him the national high school player of the year. He could turn a program around.

Not everyone was convinced about Emmitt. A well-known scout named Max Emfinger wrote for a recruiting service that at 5 feet 10 inches and 185 pounds, and with 4.6 speed in the 40-yard dash, Emmitt wouldn't be able to dodge college defenders. "Emmitt Smith isn't big or fast, and he can't get around the corner," the scout wrote. "I know all the folks in Pensacola will be screaming, and all the Florida fans will be writing me nasty letters, but

Emmitt Smith is not a franchise player. He's a lugger, not a runner. The sportswriters blew him out of proportion."[1]

The word *lugger* hit Emmitt like a punch to the gut. He was hurt and determined to prove the scout wrong.

It was hard for Emmitt to concentrate on his studies. He would sometimes get more than ten phone calls a night from recruiters. Still, Emmitt finished in the top 100 in his class academically. He knew he must study in order to go to college.

Florida State coach Bobby Bowden and Auburn coach Pat Dye even visited Emmitt's house on North G Street. That was worth taking time out from his studies.

Emmitt soon began making trips to college campuses. He visited Auburn, Nebraska, Clemson, Alabama, Florida State, and Florida. All were football powerhouses.

Eventually he narrowed his choices to two—Auburn and Florida. Auburn University was ninety miles away in southern Alabama, so it would be easy for Emmitt's family and friends to see him play. Bo Jackson had won the Heisman Trophy with the Tigers a year earlier, and Emmitt met Bo on his recruiting trip. Emmitt was impressed. He liked the idea of playing tailback in the Auburn offense. On the other hand, University of Florida in Gainesville was 300 miles away. The Florida football field was artificial turf, instead of grass like Auburn. Finally, the Gators were just coming off probation. But Florida was academically respected, and Emmitt's mother hoped he would go there.

Emmitt chose Florida.

He arrived at Gainesville one rainy day and went right to work. He pumped iron every day in the weight room and put on fifteen pounds of muscle before the season even started. The first game would be at the University of Miami, and Emmitt wanted to be ready. Coach Galen Hall had told him on his recruiting trip that if he came to Florida he would be the starting tailback.

The game at the Orange Bowl began, but Emmitt was kept on the sideline. Wayne Williams was the starting tailback. Emmitt didn't understand it. Then Florida fell behind early and abandoned the run. Emmitt didn't even get in the game until the fourth quarter. The Gators got drubbed, 31–4.

Coach Hall explained to Emmitt in practice a few days later that he did not want to put pressure on him. Emmitt insisted that he wanted the pressure. Coach Hall was pleased to hear it.

Emmitt did not start against Tulsa University the following week, either. But he did get to play more. And he was impressive. He rushed for 109

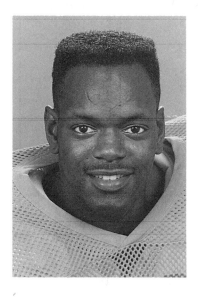

Both the University of Florida and Auburn University are national collegiate football powerhouses. Emmitt chose Florida over Auburn based on it's academic standing.

yards in just 10 carries, including a 66-yard burst for a touchdown. It was the longest scoring run at Florida since Neal Anderson's 80-yard touchdown three years earlier.

Coach Hall pondered whether to make Emmitt the starting tailback. After all, he did promise the freshman a starting position. And Emmitt looked good against Tulsa. Of course, Tulsa was not known for its defense. Florida's upcoming opponent certainly was.

Florida's next game was against mighty Alabama—in Tuscaloosa—on national TV. All sorts of things could go terribly wrong for a freshman starting his first game in dangerous enemy territory. Coach Hall couldn't decide whether to start Emmitt. Finally he made up his mind. Inside the Gators' locker room, fifteen minutes before kickoff, Coach Hall announced the starting lineups. Emmitt would be the tailback.

It was a wise decision. Emmitt cut and slashed through the Crimson Tide defense as if he were still playing in high school. The Alabama fans wondered—Who was this No. 22? Emmitt carried the ball 39 times for 224 yards. He scored 2 touchdowns as Florida pulled the upset, 23–14.

The Alabama coaches could hardly believe their eyes. "He's very deceiving," Tide Coach Bill Curry said afterward. "It's like when Herschel Walker played. Emmitt's not that big, but he's so powerful and has that deceiving style. He shuffles his feet and makes tacklers miss him. You can't practice the way he runs."[2]

Coach Hall explained why he hadn't used Emmitt more in the season opener against powerful Miami. "There's a great mental adjustment between high school and college," the coach said. "A kid like Emmitt has the ability, but I still wondered. Maybe he was there already. Maybe he just needed the chance."[3]

It didn't matter now. Emmitt was off and running. His instant success prompted sophomore teammate Octavius Gould to transfer immediately to the University of Minnesota. Gould was a high school All-America running back, but knew he had little chance of playing for the Gators now. "I tried to convince him to stay," Emmitt said. "I told him we'd need more than one tailback. But he made it clear he was transferring because of me."[4]

Emmitt rolled on. A week later against Mississippi State, he rushed for 173 yards on 20 carries and scored 3 touchdowns in a 38–3 win. The Bulldogs didn't know what hit them.

"One time in the second half he came through a hole, and I was right there waiting for him," Mississippi

State defensive tackle Anthony Butts said. "I'm not sure what he did, but the next thing I saw, he was gone."[5]

The following week, Emmitt rushed for 184 yards against LSU. Next he ran for 130 yards against Cal State-Fullerton, then 175 yards against Temple. Just like that, in seven games, Emmitt had passed the 1,000-yard mark.

At the beginning of the year, Gators quarterback Kerwin Bell was being touted for the Heisman Trophy—annually awarded to the best player in college football. Emmitt had marveled at Bell in early-season practices. Now Bell was marveling at Emmitt. "He's always looking around. He has the great vision that all the great ones have," the quarterback said. "Just standing behind him, I can see how he sets up his blockers, and how he sets up the defensive players. It's amazing."[6]

The Gators' defensive players were equally impressed. "It does something inside me to see Emmitt run," defensive tackle Henry Brown said. "If I could, I'd steal the Heisman Trophy and give it to him. He deserves it."[7]

Some eighteen-year-olds would not have handled such praise. They would have gotten a swelled head. Emmitt responded just as his parents raised him to. He remained humble. "I think I'm a good running back," he confessed. "But I'm a long way from being a great one. I'm just a freshman and I'm still learning."[8]

Florida was 5–2 when it came up against the sturdy Auburn defense. Emmitt learned the difficulty of trying to run against a powerful eight-man college front. The Tigers focused on stopping him, and they managed to slow him down, anyway. Emmitt gained just 72 yards on 21 carries as the Gators lost, 29–6. It was his first game rushing for less than one hundred yards as a starter since his sophomore year in high school. The Gators went on to lose two of their last three games to finish with a 6–5 record. They played in the Aloha Bowl against UCLA. Although the Gators lost, 20–16, it was a fun time for Emmitt. He got to meet some UCLA players who later would become his Dallas Cowboys teammates—Troy Aikman, James Washington, and Ken Norton, Jr.

Emmitt served notice his freshman season. He was a force to be reckoned with. He had 1,341 yards rushing, eight 100-yard games, and a 5.9 yards-per-carry average. He finished ninth in voting for the Heisman Trophy, just the second freshman ever to be in the top 10 in balloting. (Herschel Walker was the other.)

The eight players who finished ahead of Emmitt

in the Heisman voting, including Tim Brown of Notre Dame who won the award, departed for the pros. This made Emmitt the instant favorite as a sophomore.

Three months before Emmitt's second season began, he posed with the Heisman statue on Florida's field. He was asked to explain his secret to running. Emmitt said: "When I line up, I don't see the wide receivers or the cornerbacks, but I see everybody else on both teams. It's not a blur, but a clear picture. I probably see things other people don't see. I can see changes in coverage. I can usually look at a defense and see where the hole will be, regardless of where the play was called."[9]

Emmitt prepared well for his second college season. He cut his time in the 40-yard-dash to 4.55. He reached new maxes in the Florida weight room—leg-pressing 800 pounds and bench-pressing 305.

But he couldn't prepare for two things: a coaching change and an injury. First, the Gators hired a new offensive coordinator who switched the scheme to a passing offense. Emmitt had led the Southeastern Conference in rushing as a freshman, and quarterback Kerwin Bell had graduated. Yet the coach was switching to a passing offense.

Then Emmitt got hurt.

After five straight wins to start the season, and Emmitt breaking the 100-yard mark in all five games, the Gators came up against Memphis State. Emmitt got hit by a defensive lineman on a running play up the middle, then got crunched on the knee from behind. He crumpled to the ground.

The injury was serious. Emmitt had suffered ligament damage. The doctor told him he would miss at least a month of football, maybe even the rest of the season. Emmitt was crushed. His Heisman Trophy hopes were gone. So were Florida's chances for an undefeated season.

The Gators began to lose. Emmitt worked out each day in a swimming pool to rehabilitate his knee. He wanted to get back on the field to help his team. Florida had lost three straight games when Emmitt decided to test the knee. He convinced his coaches he was ready to return. They let him play the following week against Georgia. Emmitt wore a brace, and the knee held up fine. The Gators didn't. They lost, 26–3.

Still, Emmitt was back. He gained 68 yards against Georgia, then rushed for 113 yards the following week in a win over Kentucky. But the Gators ran into All-America Deion Sanders and the Florida State Seminoles the last week of the season and got clobbered, 52–17.

Emmitt finished the season on a high note by ripping through Illinois for 159 yards in the All-America Bowl. The Gators won, 14–10, and Emmitt was named the game's MVP. Still, he was relieved his sophomore year had ended. It was the first time in his life that football wasn't fun.

The situation at Florida grew worse the following year. The Gators were being investigated by the NCAA for recruiting violations. Coach Galen Hall abruptly resigned. Starting quarterback Kyle Morris was suspended. Through it all, Emmitt remained focused.

The Gators were 4–1 when Coach Hall resigned. They had just won a big game in the final seconds at LSU. The offense was averaging 26 points a game and the defense was ranked second in the country. It was a terrible time for Coach Hall to leave. It turned out that Hall had committed a few minor violations—enough for him to resign and for the program to be placed on probation the following year.

New offensive coordinator Whitey Jordan had designed a scheme to get Emmitt the ball more. Jordan had coached the "Pony Express" backfield of Eric Dickerson and Craig James at Southern Methodist University. He liked a running offense. And Emmitt liked Coach Jordan.

Florida Gator Emmitt Smith charges downfield. Looking toward on-coming linebackers, Smith searches for a clear path.

FACT

Emmitt played only three years at the University of Florida—opting to turn pro before his senior year. Three years was still enough time for him to break fifty-eight school records.

Emmitt even broke a Florida record the first game he started. He rushed for 224 yards against Alabama, the most yards ever gained in a game by a Florida running back. The old mark was set in 1930, nearly forty years before Emmitt was born.

Against Vanderbilt Emmitt ran like a madman. He gained 119 yards in the first half and finished with 205 as the Gators triumphed, 34–11.

"Emmitt doesn't have an ego problem," Coach Jordan said. "The No. 1 thing he's interested in is helping this football team. You can handle things when you're that way. Nothing bothers Emmitt."[10]

It was a bright October day in Gainesville the following Saturday when the Gators met the University of New Mexico. Before the sun had set, Emmitt had enjoyed his best football game ever. In a 27–21 Gators victory, Emmitt ripped and slashed through the Lobos' defense thirty-one times on the ground. When it was over, he had amassed 316 yards.

"I don't think I've ever seen a guy like Emmitt Smith in person," was all New Mexico Coach Mike Sheppard could say.[11]

Emmitt's seventy-two-yard touchdown dash in the second quarter moved him past Neal Anderson as the top rusher in Gators' history. By the end of the day, Emmitt had wiped out fourteen school records and one conference mark.

The game also marked another turning point in Emmitt's college career. Rumors began to circulate that he would skip his senior year and turn pro. The 1990 draft would be the first year in which NFL teams could select players other than seniors. Would Emmitt declare himself eligible for the draft? "I'm not going to really commit myself," Emmitt said. "I've got a lot more important things on my mind right now than skipping my senior year."[12]

But the Gators lost their last three regular season games, lost to Washington in the Freedom Bowl, and then the entire coaching staff resigned. Finally, the program was placed on NCAA probation. It would be banned from TV and bowl games. Emmitt didn't wait to make up his mind.

He was going pro.

Chapter 4

A Rookie Cowboy

Thirty-eight underclassmen declared themselves eligible for the 1990 NFL draft. Along with the usual crop of college seniors, it was a pool rich with talent.

Emmitt didn't know when he would be picked in the draft. Some scouts were predicting early in the first round. Others, who weren't satisfied with his size or speed, were figuring the second round. Emmitt had set fifty-eight school records while at the University of Florida, but some people still weren't convinced.

Emmitt watched the draft with his family on television at a friend's house at Pensacola Beach. He was so nervous he could barely focus. Illinois quarterback Jeff George went first to the Indianapolis Colts. Penn State running back Blair Thomas went next to the New York Jets. The next four picks were defensive players—Cortez Kennedy to the Seattle

Seahawks, Keith McCants to the Tampa Bay Buccaneers, Junior Seau to the San Diego Chargers, and Mark Carrier to the Chicago Bears. More teams kept with the defensive theme. Twelve of the first sixteen picks were defensive players.

The Dallas Cowboys went into the draft intent on improving their defense. But they couldn't believe Emmitt Smith was still available. Cowboys backfield coach Joe Brodsky had checked out Emmitt in Gainesville a month earlier and liked what he saw. Cowboys head coach Jimmy Johnson asked Brodsky about Emmitt's speed. "He'll take your breath away," Brodsky told Johnson, "and you won't get it back until he scores."[1]

Dallas had the twenty-first pick. Could Emmitt last until then? The Cowboys weren't willing to wait around and find out. They quickly called the Pittsburgh Steelers, who owned the seventeenth pick, and began talking trade.

Meanwhile, Emmitt could no longer bear to watch. He was outside pacing nervously. Thoughts filled his head. Maybe he shouldn't have left college early. Maybe he wouldn't get picked until late in the draft. Maybe he wouldn't get drafted at all. Then he heard his mother calling for him. He had a telephone call, she said.

Emmitt answered the phone. The voice on the

Dallas Cowboys coach Jimmy Johnson first made a name for himself at the University of Miami, where he led his football team to two consecutive Orange Bowl victories in 1987 and 1988.

other end said, "This is Bob Ackles, player personnel director of the Dallas Cowboys. Emmitt, how would you like to be a Dallas Cowboy?"

Emmitt couldn't believe it. "I'd *love* to be a Dallas Cowboy," he said.[2] Ackles said the Cowboys would call back shortly.

Dallas traded up to get Pittsburgh's pick at No. 17. Then the phone rang again. Emmitt heard Jimmy Johnson's voice on the other end. "Emmitt," Coach Johnson said, "how would you like to wear a star on your helmet?"

Emmitt was stunned. He just repeated Johnson's words. "Coach, I'd *love* to wear a star on my helmet."

"Good. Because we're about to draft you. Be ready. We'll call you back in a few minutes."

Emmitt hung up the phone and announced to everyone: "That was the Cowboys again! They say they're about to draft me!"[3]

The room erupted with cheers. Then everyone watched on television as the pick was announced by NFL Commissioner Paul Tagliabue: "The Dallas Cowboys, with the 17th pick in the 1990 NFL draft, select Emmitt Smith, running back, University of Florida."[4]

The Cowboys almost didn't get Emmitt. The Atlanta Falcons had the same idea. But the Falcons called the Steelers just seconds after the Cowboys did. When the Falcons found out the Steelers traded the seventeenth pick to the Cowboys, they called the Cowboys. Falcons vice president of player personnel Ken Herock talked with Coach Johnson. "What can we give you for your pick?" Herock asked Johnson. When Herock was told the Cowboys planned to pick Emmitt, he asked Coach Johnson, "Well, what can we give you for Emmitt Smith?" Coach Johnson just laughed.[5]

The Cowboys had finished 1–15 the year before. They ranked last in the NFC in rushing yardage. Emmitt seemed like a perfect fit. Some "experts" were skeptical, but Coach Johnson didn't care. "There were all these people saying, 'He's too slow,' or 'He's too small,'" Johnson said. "All I know is that every time I saw a film of him, he was running 50, 60, 70, 80 yards for a touchdown. That looked pretty good to me."[6]

Emmitt started learning the offense at the team's quarterback camps. Meanwhile, his agent Richard Howell began negotiating a contract. Before long, the agent and Cowboys owner Jerry Jones were locked in a bitter dispute. It took several months to get it resolved.

Emmitt was frustrated. He wanted to play football. But he also wanted to be paid fairly, and he didn't think the Cowboys were offering enough. He missed the entire preseason as the two sides haggled over money. Finally, five days before opening day, an agreement was reached: $3 million over three years.

Dallas opened the 1990 season at home against the San Diego Chargers. Emmitt stood on the sideline most of the day. Alonzo Highsmith was the starting tailback. Emmitt only got to carry the ball twice in the game. He gained just two yards. Not exactly a rousing NFL debut. At least the Cowboys won the game, 17–14.

Emmitt got to start the next week at home against the New York Giants. Things would certainly be different this time. But against the tenacious Giants' defense led by All-Pro linebacker Lawrence Taylor, Emmitt ran the ball just six times for eleven yards. The Cowboys lost, 28–7.

Emmitt told Coach Johnson to give him the ball more. He told backfield Coach Brodsky the same thing. He told anyone who would listen. Someone must have heard him. At RFK Stadium against the Washington Redskins in week three, Dallas attacked on the ground. They controlled the ball and kept it away from Washington offense. In fact, the Redskins' offense didn't score a touchdown all day. The trouble was, the defense did. Cornerback

Darrell Green intercepted a Troy Aikman pass deep in Dallas territory and skipped eighteen yards for the score. Chip Lohmiller nailed four field goals, and the Cowboys trailed 19–6. But Dallas rallied through the air. Aikman completed ten of eleven passes on a sixty-two-yard drive, and then Emmitt scored his first professional touchdown—a two-yard run. Emmitt had 17 carries for 63 yards to that point. The Cowboys were back in the game, 19–13. But time was running out. Redskins quarterback Mark Rypien had been injured since the second quarter, and backup Stan Humphries was sacked on third down by Ken Norton, Jr., at the Washington two. Then Ralf Mojsiejenko intentionally ran out of the back of the end zone with the ball for a safety. Dallas was within four points. But Emmitt never touched the ball again. Aikman threw an interception on the final drive to ruin Dallas's chances.

Afterward, there was plenty of praise for Emmitt. "Awesome—there's just one word to describe him," Redskins defensive end Fred Stokes said. "He was *awesome*."[7]

Two weeks later against the Tampa Bay Buccaneers, Emmitt put on a show in front of the home crowd. He danced and darted through the Bucs for 123 yards on 23 carries. But the outcome was still in doubt until Emmitt scooted fourteen yards for a touchdown in the fourth quarter. The Cowboys won, 14–10.

Writers began singing praises for Emmitt's running style. "Frantic hopscotching, barefoot, on a blistering sidewalk," was the way columnist Blackie Sherrod described it. "He darts, feints, shifts back and forth," wrote Jere Longman of the *Philadelphia Inquirer*. "He stops in the hole—comes to a complete stop—looks unhurriedly for a seam and skates across the field like a hot dog wrapper."[8]

Just as quickly as the Cowboys turned to Emmitt to lead their offense, though, they turned away from him. In the next five games, Emmitt carried the ball just twelve, sixteen, fourteen, fifteen, and six times. The Cowboys lost four of those games. Emmitt insisted that he needed the ball more to take the pressure off Aikman.

Again, someone listened. Against the Los Angeles Rams, Emmitt got 21 carries. Although he only gained 54 yards, he opened up the passing lanes for his quarterback. Even Emmitt got into the receiving act, catching 4 passes for 117 yards. The Cowboys won.

The next week against the Redskins, Emmitt carried 23 times for 132 yards and 2 touchdowns. The Cowboys won again.

FACT

When Emmitt left the University of Florida after his junior year to turn pro, he did not officially graduate from college. Emmitt still had thirteen units to go to obtain his degree. His mother, Mary, made a deal with Emmitt. Emmitt could not buy his own house until he went back to finish his degree. Even though Emmitt is a millionaire now, he has held true to his deal. He still lives at home and plans to get his degree soon.

His rookie year complete, Smith went on to play in the Pro Bowl. He was the only Cowboy chosen that year.

The following week against the New Orleans Saints, Emmitt ran 20 times for 85 yards and a touchdown. The Cowboys won again.

Then against the Phoenix Cardinals, Emmitt carried 24 times for 103 yards and 4 touchdowns. On one play, he took the handoff, fell down, got up, and still scored from six yards out. The Cowboys won again.

Dallas had improved to 7–7 and was hoping for a wild card berth. But the offensive coordinator mysteriously abandoned the run again the final two games. Emmitt carried just fourteen and sixteen times. The Cowboys lost both games.

It was a strange and exciting first year for Emmitt, who amassed 937 yards rushing and was honored as the NFL's Rookie of the Year. He also made the Pro Bowl—a rare feat by a rookie. The Cowboys won six more games than they had the previous season, and Jimmy Johnson was named Coach of the Year. But Emmitt and the team expected more. They didn't like losing. They wanted to make the playoffs. They would have to wait until the following year.

Chapter 5

Moving Up

It had to change. Jimmy Johnson knew it. Emmitt Smith knew it. The entire Dallas organization knew it. So Johnson did what he had to do. He made the change. Coach Johnson fired offensive coordinator David Shula in February and replaced him with Norv Turner. Norv who?

That's what Emmitt wanted to know. He had never met Norv Turner. All Emmitt knew was that this would be his seventh offensive coordinator in seven years, dating clear back to his junior year in high school. It seemed he always had to learn a new playbook. Emmitt would come to love Turner's playbook.

The Cowboys arrived at Cleveland Municipal Stadium for the 1991 season opener against the Browns. Cleveland is one of the toughest places on the road to play because the fans in the Dawg

Coach Jimmy Johnson and Emmitt Smith share a light moment together during practice.

FACT

Former Cowboys running back Tony Dorsett is third on the all-time career rushing list. But in a dozen seasons, Dorsett never once led the league in rushing. A Cowboys jinx? Hardly.

Not only did Emmitt become the first Cowboy to win the NFL rushing title when he gained 1,563 yards in 1991, but he cleared the 1,500 mark younger than anyone in pro football history. Emmitt was just twenty-two years and seven months old when he accomplished the feat.

Pound are so crazy. But the Cowboys didn't let the noise get to them. They came out charging.

Dallas chewed more than six minutes off the clock on its opening possession by throwing short passes and plowing Emmitt up the middle. Ken Willis kicked a thirty-eight-yard field goal to give the Cowboys a 3–0 lead.

Cleveland answered with a touchdown on Kevin Mack's one-yard plunge. The drive was aided by a thirty-two-yard interference call against the Cowboys.

Dallas trailed, 7–3, but didn't deviate from its plan. Aikman moved the ball with quick passes, and Emmitt ate up more yardage on the ground. Willis kicked another field goal to close the gap to one point, 7–6. The drive lasted sixteen plays and took more than eight and a half minutes.

The next time the Cowboys got the ball, they didn't stop rolling until they reached the end zone. Aikman passed three yards to tight end Jay Novacek for the score. Now Dallas led, 13–7.

Dallas took possession one last time before the half and marched again. This time it was an eleven-play drive. And the result was the same—another score. Aikman connected with wideout Michael Irvin for a four-yard touchdown. Emmitt kept the drive alive by scampering twelve yards on a third-and-ten play.

For the half, the Cowboys ran forty-three offensive plays. Twenty-one of them involved Emmitt. Already he had rushed for 72 yards. And he had four catches for 26 more. Most important, Dallas led, 20–7.

The Browns struck back. On the first play of the second half, quarterback Bernie Kosar hit receiver Webster Slaughter on a sixty-two-yard bomb for a touchdown. Cleveland trailed by six, 20–14.

Dallas kept with its game plan. The offensive line, led by center Mark Stepnoski and tackle Nate Newton, opened holes for Emmitt. The Cowboys maintained possession for much of the second half. Two of the drives resulted in field goals. Cleveland didn't score again, and Dallas won the game, 26–14.

Emmitt had pounded the Browns for 112 yards on the ground and caught six passes for 36 more. "We had the ball an awful lot, didn't we?" Emmitt said in a locker room interview. "I knew I'd be getting the ball a lot, but I didn't expect they'd give it to me 32 times. Man, I'm going to feel it tomorrow."[1]

The Cowboys picked up where they left off in week two. This time, it was in front of a national television audience on Monday Night Football. The Washington Redskins traveled to Dallas to try to stop the new offensive machine. The Redskins couldn't. But Dallas couldn't stop Washington's offense either, and the game became a shootout.

The Cowboys took an early 7–0 lead on one of those long, time-consuming drives again. Aikman passed three yards to Novacek to cap the eighty-yard, eleven-play drive. But the Redskins recovered a fumbled punt and went twenty-five yards in three plays to tie it, 7–7. It didn't stay tied for long. In a great TV highlight burst, Emmitt took a handoff around left end, slipped three arm tackles, and outraced free safety Brad Edwards and linebacker Andre Collins seventy-five yards for a touchdown. At the end of the first quarter, Emmitt had 5 carries for 104 yards, and Dallas led, 14–7.

But Emmitt's stomach was bothering him. Before the game, he had told fullback Daryl "Moose" Johnston that he was concerned about getting tired. It was a warm Dallas evening, and Emmitt figured to carry the ball often. Johnston said he knew what to do. He fixed Emmitt a powdered drink. It was a powdered food supplement mixed with water that Johnston drank before every game. He handed it to Emmitt. It looked terrible. It tasted even worse. Emmitt drank it down.

When Emmitt reached the end zone after his seventy-five-yard touchdown, his stomach starting spinning. Emmitt felt like he was going to get sick.

Emmitt Smith sails down a clear field.

He walked over to the Cowboys' bench, and then he *did* get sick—right on national TV.

Emmitt felt lousy after that. Needless to say, he didn't carry the ball much. He only gained eight yards on six carries the rest of the night. Dallas lost, 33–31.

The Eagles came to town the following week and clobbered the Cowboys, 24–0. Coach Johnson was irate. So were the players. Not only did they lose at home to an NFC East foe, they got humiliated. Practices were extra hard that week. It was time to get in gear. The opening-day victory in Cleveland was long forgotten.

In Phoenix against the Cardinals, Emmitt had his biggest day yet as a Cowboy. On the third play of the game, he took a handoff up the middle, cut left, and raced sixty yards for a score. The Cowboys never trailed in the game. Emmitt scored another touchdown and finished with 182 yards rushing as Dallas won, 17–9. After the game, Troy Aikman was asked about Emmitt. "Being on the field, being behind him and having some idea of what he's seeing—it's really amazing some of the things he does," Aikman said. "I don't do a good job carrying out fakes because I enjoy watching him run so much."[2]

The Cowboys were cooking now. After beating

the Cardinals, they knocked off the Giants, the Green Bay Packers, and the Cincinnati Bengals, posting a 5–2 record. Emmitt had carried for 589 yards which put him at the top of the league rushing list. He was on his way to meeting a goal he had set for himself when the season began—to win the NFL rushing title.

The Cowboys lost three of their next four games, but finished with a flourish in winning their last five. They did it without Troy Aikman who missed the last four games with an injury. Backup Steve Beuerlein filled in nicely, but the load fell on the shoulders of Emmitt Smith. And, as expected, Emmitt came through. First, in a 24–21 win at Washington, Emmitt carried 34 times for 132 hard-earned yards. The Redskins would go on to win the Super Bowl that year largely because of their defensive front. Emmitt was the only running back to run for over 100 yards against them. And he did it twice!

On Thanksgiving Day, Emmitt powered for 109 yards against the tough Pittsburgh Steelers. Then he became the only back to gain more than 100 against the rock solid New Orleans Saints when he ripped them for 112. Emmitt closed the season with a stirring 160-yard performance against the Atlanta Falcons. For the season, he had collected 1,593 yards or 365 carries—enough to edge out Barry Sanders and Thurman Thomas for the NFL rushing title. Emmitt was thrilled, but he had very little time to celebrate. The Cowboys were headed to the playoffs.

Emmitt didn't know what NFL playoff pressure felt like. Sure, he had been in the playoffs in high school, but this was a little different. Most of his teammates felt the same way. Only eleven Cowboys had been in a playoff game. It was all new to the coaches as well. To make matters worse, Dallas was a wild card entry and it had to play on the frozen tundra of Chicago's Soldier Field.

If the Cowboys were nervous, they didn't show it. They took a 3–0 lead on their first possession as Ken Willis nailed a twenty-seven-yard field goal. Emmitt made the big play of the drive—a nineteen-yard burst up the middle. He almost made a bonehead play, too, when he was stripped of the ball by Chicago lineman Richard Dent. But Emmitt managed to recover his fumble at the Bears' twelve to give Willis a shot at the field goal. The Cowboys scored again on their next possession, but this time it was a touchdown. Derrick Brownlow blocked a punt and Ken Norton, Jr., recovered at the Bears' ten. Five plays later, Emmitt banged in from the one. Dallas led, 10–0.

The Bears responded with two field goals, but

the Cowboys scored a touchdown in the third quarter to ice the game. Beuerlein hit Novacek for a three-yard score to cap a seventy-five-yard drive led mostly by Emmitt's running. He churned through the Chicago defense for runs of eleven, ten, eight, seven, five, and three yards. Emmitt ran up the middle on one play, and hard-hitting safety Mark Carrier came up to meet him. Emmitt drove Carrier back several yards with an upper-cut forearm to the chest.

The Bears scored a touchdown with two minutes left but didn't come close again. The Cowboys triumphed, 17–13.

"I enjoyed the field even though it was in bad shape," Emmitt said afterward. "I thought it was to my advantage. Some guys lost footing, but I was able to cut. I can go the other direction in one step."[3] The Bears found that out.

Everything came crashing to a halt for the Cowboys the following week in Detroit. The game was billed as a showdown between Emmitt and Detroit's Barry Sanders. Emmitt won that battle with 80 yards rushing to 69 for Sanders, but the Cowboys lost the game. Lost it badly. Lions quarterback Erik Kramer riddled the Dallas secondary for 29 completions and 341 yards as Detroit won in a rout, 38–6. "We just played terrible," said Emmitt, who got to

FACT

No running back had ever gained 100 yards against the Chicago Bears in the playoffs. Not at home. Not on the road. The record dated back to 1932 and spanned twenty-seven games. Emmitt Smith arrived at frigid Soldier Field in Chicago in late December to play in his first NFL playoff game. Emmitt darted through the Bears' defense for 105 yards to snap the sixty-year-old streak. Dallas won the game, 17–13.

Emmitt goes over the top against the Broncos.

carry the ball just three times in the second half. "We couldn't sustain anything consistently."[4]

It was a humbling experience for the young Cowboys, but it made them hungrier, too. They liked the taste of these NFL playoffs. They would soon get a bellyful.

Chapter 6

Rushing Leader

Emmitt was the only Cowboy to go to Hawaii after his rookie season. But he didn't make the trip to the Pro Bowl alone his second time. Emmitt was joined by three offensive teammates—Troy Aikman, Michael Irvin, and Jay Novacek. Aikman led the league in passing before getting hurt, Irvin led the league in receiving yardage, and Novacek led all tight ends in receptions. And Emmitt, of course, led the league in rushing. It was a glimpse of what was to come in Emmitt's third year with the Cowboys— the stirring Super Bowl season of 1992–93.

The Cowboys couldn't have opened the season in a bigger way. With a national television audience tuned in to ABC's Monday Night Football, Dallas clubbed the Washington Redskins—defending Super Bowl champions—23–10.

The Cowboys dominated throughout. They outgained Washington 279 yards to 111—in the *first half.* Michael Irvin finished with five catches for eighty-nine yards. Wideout Alvin Harper scored the second touchdown of his career. New defensive end Charles Haley, acquired in the off-season from the San Francisco 49ers, harassed Super Bowl XXVI MVP quarterback Mark Rypien. But the big news was Emmitt Smith. Emmitt rushed 27 times for 140 yards and a touchdown. It was the fourth straight time Emmitt had broken the 100-yard mark against the Redskins. No running back in history had accomplished that. "I think we're getting better," is all Jimmy Johnson said.[1] The Cowboys were on a mission this year.

The Cowboys went to Giants Stadium six days later and took a commanding 34–0 lead against the Giants. The Cowboys were good, but they didn't know they were *this* good. Maybe they were better than they thought. So they relaxed. And they nearly got beat. The Giants scored four straight touchdowns to close to within six, 34–28. But the rally fell short and Dallas held on. A win is a win, but no one felt good about the way it almost turned out.

After splitting its next two games, Dallas reeled off five straight victories. Among them were an impressive win at the Los Angeles Memorial Coliseum over the Raiders and a victory over the hated rival Philadelphia Eagles.

Teammates Michael Irvin and Emmitt Smith walk off the field together. The Cowboys had a stranglehold on yardage titles in 1991. Irvin led the NFL in receiving yardage, while Smith led the league in rushing.

On a sunny day in Los Angeles, Emmitt actually outgained the entire Raiders offense. He scored from the six yard line behind Novacek's block on the right side to put the Cowboys ahead, 7–6, in the first quarter. Then, three plays afer Aikman completed a fifty-two-yard pass to Harper, Emmitt ran four yards into the end zone off the right side to make it 14–13 in the third quarter. Finally, against an eight-man defensive front and an all-out blitz, Emmitt burst through for a twenty-six-yard touchdown to clinch the 28–13 win. "It's easy to call winning plays when he's in the game," offensive coordinator Turner said in the locker room. "When you're in doubt, it's not a bad idea to give Emmitt the ball."[2]

The Philadelphia Eagles came to town with a streak of not allowing a 100-yard runner for 53 games. Emmitt took care of that. He rushed for over 100 yards—in the *second half*. Emmitt gained 53 yards in the first two quarters, then piled up 110 in the next two, for a total of 163 yards, as Dallas plucked the Eagles, 20–10. The win gave the Cowboys a two-game lead in the tough NFC East at the halfway point of the year. "That doesn't necessarily mean anything," warned Emmitt. "That just means we can't afford any letdowns."[3]

The Cowboys coasted the rest of the regular

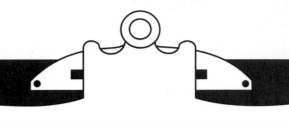

STATS

Emmitt gave each of his offensive lineman a Rolex watch when he won his first rushing title. When he did it again the next year, he gave them each a painting.

No.	Player	Pos.	Ht.	Wt.	College
Starter					
71	Mark Tuinei	LT	6' 5"	305	Hawaii
61	Nate Newton	LG	6' 3"	325	Florida A&M
53	Mark Stepnoski	C	6' 2"	269	Pittsburgh
60	Derek Kennard	RG	6' 3"	300	Nevada Reno
79	Erik Williams	RT	6' 6"	324	Central State, Ohio
Key Reserves					
68	Frank Cornish	C	6' 4"	287	UCLA
70	Dale Hellestrae	G	6' 5"	275	SMU
73	Larry Allen	T	6' 3"	325	Sonoma State

season, winning five of their last seven games, and clinching the NFC East title at the Georgia Dome in Atlanta. There were plenty of stars for the Cowboys, but, once again, Emmitt stole the show. He rushed for 132 yards after halftime and set a team record for touchdowns in a season with his 17th and 18th. The Cowboys won in a rout, 41–17. "This is something that we've worked hard for all year," Emmitt said, "but we can't stop now."[4] Nobody could stop them, either.

Emmitt closed the regular season with 131 yards against the Bears and 1,713 on the season for his second straight rushing title. He edged out Pittsburgh's Barry Foster for the title, and it felt just as good as the first one.

The Cowboys rolled into the playoffs with momentum. And they rolled right over the Eagles in the opening round, 34–10, as Emmitt broke their backs with a 23-yard scoring burst on a draw play among his 114 rushing yards. No time to celebrate now. Up next were the San Francisco 49ers.

If there was one team that had a chance against the Cowboys, it was the 49ers. San Francisco had been to four Super Bowls in the 1980s and won all four. The Niners had compiled the best record in the NFL again in 1992 with the passing of league MVP Steve Young, the catching of future Hall-of-Famer

Jerry Rice, and the running of Ricky Watters. Really, the 49ers were similar to the Cowboys in most ways. But there were two noticable differences between the teams: the Cowboys had a better defense, and the Cowboys had Emmitt Smith.

The 49ers had the home-field advantage, however, and it had been raining all week in the Bay Area. The Candlestick Park field was a soggy mess, even though 23,000 square feet of new sod had been carted in several days before the big game. One local San Francisco columnist wrote: "The Cowboys play in pretty, carpeted Texas Stadium. Get them into a good mud puddle and they might panic."[5]

This was the NFC Championship Game. The winner would go to the Super Bowl. The Cowboys had come so far. They weren't about to panic now.

San Francisco struck on its first play of the game. Young dropped back and threw a perfect pass to Rice for a sixty-three-yard touchdown bomb. There was only one problem: the officials called it back. They penalized the 49ers ten yards for holding and wiped out the score. Still, San Francisco drove for a score to take a 7–0 lead before Dallas answered with a field goal. Then the Cowboys got another break. On third-and-goal at the San Francisco seven yard line, Aikman couldn't find a receiver open and threw the ball away. Just as he did, 49ers lineman

Pierce Holt whacked Emmitt to the turf. The referee called pass interference on Holt, giving the Cowboys new life. Emmitt ran it in from the two to give Dallas a 10–7 lead. The 49ers tied it with a field goal before the half.

The Cowboys took control in the second half. They drove seventy-eight yards for a touchdown to make it 17–10. After the 49ers kicked a field goal, the Cowboys drove seventy-nine yards for another score. Again, Emmitt made the key play. On third down at the San Francisco sixteen, Emmitt swung out to the right flat to serve as a secondary receiver. Nobody covered him. Aikman spotted it and threw quickly. Emmitt caught the pass and took off. He sprinted to the right corner of the end zone and reached it before linebacker Bill Romanowski could catch him. Suddenly, Dallas was up 24–13.

With seven minutes to play, Young drove the 49ers in the hurry-up offense ninety-three yards for a score. It was 24–20. There were still four minutes and twenty-two seconds left. That's when offensive coordinator Turner made the call of the game. Instead of trying to run the ball to move the clock as the 49ers expected, Turner called for a first-down pass. Alvin Harper ran a deep slant-in pattern. Aikman put it right on the money. Cornerback Don Griffin slipped in the mud, and Harper was off and

FACT

Emmitt spends much of his time in the off-season picking up awards and making acceptance speeches. Here are some of the awards he won in 1993:
- NFL Most Valuable Player
- Associated Press Player of the Year
- *The Sporting News* Player of the Year
- Pro Football Writers of America Award
- The ESPN "ESPY" MVP
- Bert Bell Award
- *Football Newsweekly* Offensive Player of the Year
- NFL Alumni Running Back of the Year
- Super Bowl XXVIII MVP

running. He went seventy yards until he was tackled at the nine. Emmitt plowed to the six, and then Aikman iced the game with a pass to Kelvin Martin for the touchdown. Dallas won the game, 30–20.

NFC Championship pressure? The Cowboys had played a flawless game. The 49ers committed four turnovers. The Cowboys didn't commit any. Emmitt gained 114 yards on the ground, caught 7 passes for 59 more, and scored 2 touchdowns. There wasn't a better feeling in the world for a football player. The Cowboys were going to the Super Bowl.

Chapter 7

The Show

Football players dream of someday playing in the biggest one-day sports spectacle in the world— the Super Bowl. Or, as the players refer to it, "The Show." Emmitt Smith and the Dallas Cowboys blitzed through the playoffs early in 1993 to make it to The Show.

Super Bowl XXVII was staged at the Rose Bowl in sunny Pasadena, California. Dallas's opponent would be the Buffalo Bills from the AFC. The Bills were no strangers to The Show. They had played in the previous two Super Bowls and lost both times—once to the New York Giants and once to the Washington Redskins. The Giants and Redskins were Cowboys' rivals from the NFC East—so if those teams beat the Bills, the Cowboys had better win too.

Emmitt emerged from the tunnel upon being introduced, and he was overwhelmed at the scene.

The stands were jammed with 98,374 fans—the largest crowd ever to witness a Cowboys' football game. Emmitt knew that twenty-seven friends and family were among that cheering mass. He also knew that millions more people were watching this game on television. How many millions? More than 133 million people, making it one of the most watched events in television history!

The Cowboys couldn't have started any worse. After they moved the ball just one yard on their first possession, Bills' special-teams star Steve Tasker shot through the line and blocked a punt. The Bills raced sixteen yards in four plays, with Thurman Thomas running two yards for the touchdown. Steve Christie kicked the extra point, and just like that the Bills had a 7–0 lead. But the Cowboys got a break. Thomas sprained his ankle on the touchdown run, and it would bother him the rest of the game.

The Bills got the ball back and marched to midfield. Then, suddenly, the Cowboys woke up. Safety James Washington smartly stepped in front of tight end Pete Metzelaars to intercept Jim Kelly's pass. The Cowboys offense took over. Six plays later, they were in the end zone. The Buffalo defense had studied game films and geared itself for the run. Defensive end Bruce Smith and linebacker Cornelius

FACT

In 1992, Emmitt broke another NFL record when he became the first player to lead the league in rushing and to play in the Super Bowl in the same season. Just for good measure, he did it again the following year.

Bennett focused on Emmitt in the backfield and almost ignored the passing game. The Cowboys saw this. So they passed the ball over the top, with Aikman throwing to wideouts Michael Irvin and Alvin Harper and tight end Jay Novacek. Aikman's twenty-three-yard pass to Novacek was good for the score, and the game was tied, 7–7.

Emmitt served as a decoy on that series, but it was fine with him. He would get his chance. And besides, the Cowboys were on the scoreboard.

Dallas took a 14–7 lead just seconds later when defensive end Charles Haley sacked Kelly at his two yard line, causing Kelly to fumble. Defensive tackle Jimmie Jones caught the ball out of the air and fell into the end zone for an easy score.

It got worse for Kelly. On Buffalo's next series, linebacker Ken Norton, Jr., drilled the quarterback in the knee with his helmet. Kelly was knocked from the game. Backup Frank Reich replaced him. Reich had led the Bills to a miraculous playoff comeback a month earlier when they trailed the Houston Oilers, 35–3, but won the game, 41–38. Could he do the same thing against the Cowboys?

No. After Buffalo got a field goal, Emmitt sprung free on a trap play to the right and rumbled thirty-eight yards to the Bills' nineteen. Emmitt could have scored but lost his footing on the play.

Quarterback Troy Aikman and wide receiver Michael Irvin confer on the field. When opponents' defenses covered Smith too tightly, the Cowboy's switched to a passing offense, hitting wideout Irvin.

On the next snap, Aikman zipped a pass to Irvin for the touchdown. Then Thomas fumbled, the Cowboys recovered, and Aikman connected with Irvin again for a score, this time from nineteen yards out. It was 28–10 at the half. It was over.

Aikman was at it again in the second half. He passed forty-five yards to Harper for a touchdown, then drove the Cowboys downfield again, where Emmitt finally got his moment to shine. He had been watching his teammates score all the touchdowns. He wanted one, too. On third-and-goal from the ten, offensive coordinator Norv Turner crossed the Bills up with a draw play. Emmitt knew in the huddle that this might be his last chance to score. The coaches would probably take him out after this drive. He was determined to reach that goal line. Emmitt took the handoff and broke several arm tackles. He banged into the end zone. At last, he had a Super Bowl touchdown.

The Cowboys closed the scoring on Norton's fumble recovery for a touchdown. They won by the lopsided score of 52–17.

Everyone contributed to the Dallas victory. The defense had registered a Super Bowl-record nine turnovers in the game. Emmitt had 108 yards rushing and 27 yards receiving on 6 catches. Irvin had 6 receptions for 114 yards and 2 touchdowns. But the

MVP was Aikman who completed 22 of 30 passes for 273 yards and 4 TDs.

Emmitt loved the sweet feeling of victory. Unfortunately, it didn't last very long.

Emmitt's three-year contract with the Cowboys had expired. It was time to negotiate a new contract. Emmitt's agent Richard Howell met with Cowboys owner Jerry Jones and asked for a raise—a *big* raise. Jones agreed—to a *small* raise. It was far less than Emmitt felt he was worth after three years, two rushing titles, and one Super Bowl championship. The two sides battled it out through the summer but resolved nothing. The preseason came and went. When the regular season began, Emmitt was holding out back home in Pensacola. He was prepared to sit out the year, if he had to.

"Emmitt Smith is a luxury, not a necessity for the Cowboys," Jones said.[1]

The players and coaches disagreed. They knew they needed Emmitt. It showed when the Redskins buried them, 35–16, to open the season. Emmitt watched the game from his home. He couldn't believe he wasn't helping the Cowboys. He wanted to be paid fairly, that's all.

In the mornings he would go to Escambia High and work out on the track or in the weight room. In the afternoons he would work at the memorabilia shop run by his mother and sister. At night, he would be at home spending time with his family or playing video games.

Meanwhile, the Cowboys were in trouble. They lost their second straight game—to the Buffalo Bills. Emmitt's replacement, rookie Derrick Lassic, fumbled twice. Coach Johnson was so angry with the whole situation that he couldn't even speak after the game. Jerry Jones had seen enough. He met Emmitt at a restaurant in Atlanta that night and offered him $13.6 million over four years. Emmitt signed and flew in to Dallas.

No team had ever lost the first two games of the season, then won a Super Bowl. The Cowboys would become the first.

Emmitt was better than ever. He touched the ball 419 times and fumbled it away only twice. Despite missing the first two games and averaging 86 carries less than the previous two seasons, he still rushed for 1,486 yards to win his third straight NFL rushing title. He was named Player of the Week, Player of the Month, and Player of the Year.

He was at his best when the Cowboys needed him the most. In a titanic battle at Giants Stadium in the final week of the regular season, Emmitt was a one-man wrecking crew. The game was crucial because the winner would get home field advantage

Cowboys owner Jerry Jones and coach Jimmy Johnson celebrate. After losing the first two games of the 1993 season, Jones realized how much the Cowboys need Emmitt.

throughout the playoffs. The loser would get in as a wild card.

In a bitter contest that wasn't decided until overtime, Emmitt rushed 32 times for 168 yards and caught 10 passes for 61 more. He handled the ball on 42 of the Cowboys' 70 plays. And he played the entire second half with a separated shoulder.

The injury occured on Emmitt's longest run of the day—a forty-six-yarder. He went off right tackle and broke free down the sideline. Giants safety Greg Jackson caught him deep in New York territory and drove him to the artificial turf. A pain shot up through Emmitt's shoulder. "When Emmitt didn't get up, I knew it was bad," left guard Nate Newton said. "It takes an awful lot to keep him on the ground."[2]

Emmitt was helped off the field, and the Cowboys kicked a field goal to take a 13–0 lead into the locker room at halftime. Doctors examined Emmitt's shoulder and told him it didn't look good. Emmitt insisted on playing. He wanted to win his third straight rushing title. And he had to help his team win.

The Giants rallied in the second half. They drove thirty-nine yards for a touchdown after recovering a fumbled punt and kicked two field goals to tie the game. It went to overtime. The Dallas defense held, and the offense took the field.

FACT

Football isn't the only sport Emmitt plays. "The Emmitt Smith Charity Golf Tournament" is held every March in Pensacola, Florida. Emmitt and several of his Cowboy teammates compete as celebrities each year in the event. All proceeds are donated to charity.

Emmitt's right arm dangled helplessly at his side. But he still had his left arm, and he always carries the ball in his left arm. Play after play, Aikman called Emmitt's name in the huddle. And play after play, the great running back answered the call. He carried the ball nine times in eleven plays, and gained 41 of the Cowboys' 52 yards on the drive. Kicker Eddie Murray drilled a 41-yard field goal with just over four minutes left in the overtime. Dallas won, 16–13.

After such a heroic game, there was no stopping Emmitt in the playoffs. He got two weeks of rest because the Cowboys earned a first-round bye, but his shoulder was still sore when the Green Bay Packers arrived in Dallas for a quarterfinal matchup. Emmitt was effective with 13 carries for 60 yards as the Cowboys rolled to a 27–17 win. That set up another NFC championship game showdown with the San Francisco 49ers. "We will win the ballgame," Coach Johnson guaranteed three days before the game. "And you can put it in three-inch headlines. We will win the ballgame."[3]

Emmitt hates shots. But this was a huge game, so three hours before kickoff he took a cortisone injection to help ease his shoulder pain. Then he went out and destroyed the 49ers. He handled the ball seven times in the Cowboys' first possession, scored the touchdown on a five-yard run, and never

Emmitt Smith and Coach Jimmy Johnson celebrate.

stopped. By the half, Emmitt had 144 yards total offense and 2 touchdowns, and Dallas held a commanding 28–7 lead. The Cowboys cruised to a 38–21 win, just as Coach Johnson predicted. The two men walked off the field together, player and coach, arm in arm, saluting to the cheering crowd. "I love you!" Johnson yelled to Emmitt.

"I love you, too!" Emmitt yelled back.

"You mean a lot to me, you know," Johnson shouted.

"I know," Emmitt said.[4]

Dallas beat the Bills in the Super Bowl again, and people were calling the Cowboys a dynasty. But then everything came crashing to a halt. Jimmy Johnson quit.

Chapter 8

A New Direction

Emmitt had lost his coach. Jimmy Johnson grew tired of feuding with owner Jerry Jones so he walked away. Former Oklahoma Sooners coach Barry Switzer was hired the next day. Emmitt didn't know much about Switzer. All he knew was that Johnson had built the Cowboys into a winning team. The mood was not pleasant among the two-time Super Bowl champions.

"It's not as happy as a lot of people may think it is," Emmitt said.[1]

Things got worse for Emmitt. First, he underwent surgery to repair his right shoulder. Then, a month before training camp, his grandmother Erma died. Emmitt was devastated. Football seemed so insignificant. He loved his grandmother so much. "Now that she's gone," he said, "it just makes me look back and appreciate everything that much more."[2]

Barry Switzer, former Oklahoma Sooners coach, replaced Jimmy Johnson as Dallas Cowboys coach.

Emmitt started the 1994 season with a bang. At Three Rivers Stadium in the season opener, he darted and plowed through the Pittsburgh Steelers for 171 yards and a touchdown to lead the Cowboys to a 26–9 victory. "You watch Emmitt Smith," television commentator John Madden said, "and it's like watching a man playing against boys."[3] Jimmy Johnson? Barry Switzer? It didn't seem to matter to Emmitt.

But the season did not go so smoothly after that. The Cowboys won their share of games with Emmitt carrying the load. But they lost a few, too. None was more painful than the last-second 19–14 defeat at home to the Browns. Jay Novacek took the potential game-winning pass but slipped at the one yard line as time ran out. Dallas would lose homefield advantage to the 49ers, and it would cost them.

Then, with two games left before the playoffs, disaster struck. Emmitt got hurt again. In the third quarter of a 24–16 victory at New Orleans, he felt a twinge in the back of his leg. He crumpled to the ground in pain. Emmitt had suffered a pulled hamstring. He was helped to the sideline, then taken off the field on a cart.

Emmitt did not play against the Giants in the last game of the regular season, and Dallas lost. Emmitt's string of rushing titles had ended, too.

At least the Cowboys still had the playoffs to look forward to.

The playoffs didn't go well either. After trouncing the Packers at home, Dallas traveled to San Francisco for yet another NFC title showdown. The 49ers had prepared well in the off-season, acquiring five Pro Bowl players on defense, including superstar cornerback Deion Sanders and Cowboys linebacker Ken Norton, Jr.

The 49ers jumped out to a 21–0 lead in the game's first seven minutes, and the Cowboys would never catch them. Emmitt did all he could. He ran 20 times with his sore hamstring for 74 yards and scored 2 touchdowns. But Dallas lost, 38–28, to the eventual Super Bowl XXIX champs.

"My leg is sore," Emmitt said afterward. "In fact, both my legs are sore. I pulled the other hamstring, too."[4] The sorest part of Emmitt, though, was his heart. He hugged his buddy, Michael Irvin, in the locker room, and together they cried.

During the upcoming year those tears would turn to smiles as the Cowboys captured a third Super Bowl championship in four seasons. In Super Bowl XXX the Cowboys defeated the Pittsburgh Steelers, 27–17. Smith led the league with 1,773 yards rushing, and broke the NFL record for most rushing touchdowns in a season with 25.

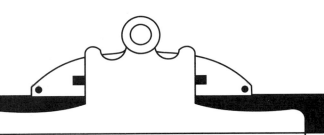

STATS

Emmitt has his sights set on the all-time career rushing record. Here is a list of the leading lifetime rushers:

Name	Yrs.	Att.	Yards	Avg.
Walter Payton	13	3,838	16,726	4.4
Eric Dickerson	11	2,996	13,259	4.4
Tony Dorsett	12	2,936	12,739	4.3
Jim Brown	9	2,359	12,312	5.2
Franco Harris	13	2,949	12,120	4.1
John Riggins	14	2,916	11,352	3.9
O.J. Simpson	11	2,404	11,236	4.7
Emmitt Smith	6	2,007	8,986	4.5

Emmitt Smith wants to be a rushing legend that future running backs will strive to catch.

"When I won the first rushing title, people wondered if I was for real and if I could do it again," Emmitt says. "Then I won the second, and they thought maybe I was for real. Then the third one made me legitimate. But now people want to know this: How long can Emmitt Smith be on top? I think I can be there a long time."[5]

Emmitt Smith will also be in Dallas for a long time. Smith's contract problems are behind him. Prior to the 1996 season he signed a new contract reported to be for $48 million over eight years.

Emmitt is driven by a fierce intensity. "There's so much more I need to accomplish," he says. "I have so much room to grow, both as a player and as a person. If you're satisfied, you're finished. You can never be satisfied."[6]

Just what does Emmitt want to accomplish? Former running back Walter Payton amassed 16,726 yards rushing in 13 seasons with the Chicago Bears. Payton is the all-time NFL rushing leader. Emmitt wants to break Payton's record.

"I'm chasing after legends, after Walter Payton and Tony Dorsett and Jim Brown and Eric Dickerson, after guys who made history," Emmitt says. "When my career's over, I want to have the new kids, the new backs, say, 'Boy, we have to chase a legend to be the best.' And they'll mean Emmitt Smith."[7]

Notes by Chapter

Chapter 1

1. Frank Litsky, "Smith Grabs Ball, Dallas Grabs Game," *The New York Times* (January 31, 1994), p. 30.

2. Ed Werder, "Emmitt Smith Has Done It All, But He Says That's Not Enough," *Dallas Morning News* (September 1, 1994), p. 1.

3. Dick Enberg, NBC-TV telecast, January 30, 1994.

4. Litsky, p. 30.

5. Enberg.

6. Bob Trumpy, NBC-TV telecast, January 30, 1994.

7. Kent Pulliam, "Emmitt Smith Asks for Ball, Then Carries It, Dallas to Win," *Kansas City Star* (January 31, 1994), p. 1.

8. Werder, p. 3.

9. Litsky, p. 1.

Chapter 2

1. David Tarrant, "Taking Care of Business On and Off the Field," *Dallas Morning News* (August 14, 1994), p. 2.

2. Steve Delsohn, *The Emmitt Zone* (New York: Crown Publishers, Inc., 1994), p. 30.

3. Jim Reeves, "For Love or Glory," *Fort Worth Star-Telegram* (July 24, 1994), p. 1.

4. Ibid.

5. Jim Reeves, "For Love or Glory," *Fort Worth Star-Telegram* (July 24, 1994), p. 1.

6. Leigh Montville, "A Man of Vision," *Sports Illustrated* (February 15, 1994), pp. 142–151.

7. Montville, p. 145.

8. Ibid.

9. Rick Telander, "Growing Up Fast," *Sports Illustrated* (November 16, 1987), p. 52.

10. Paul Zimmerman, "The 100-Yard Dasher," *Sports Illustrated* (October 21, 1991), p. 76.

Chapter 3

1. Ira Winderman, "Go-Go Gator Emmitt Smith Surprised A Lot of People," *The Sporting News* (November 30, 1987), p. 30.

2. Ibid.

3. Rick Telander, "Growing Up Fast," *Sports Illustrated* (November 16, 1987), p. 46.

4. Ibid.

5. Ibid.

6. Winderman, p. 30.

7. Telander, p. 46.

8. Winderman, p. 30.

9. Leigh Montville, "A Man of Vision," *Sports Illustrated* (February 15, 1994), p. 147.

10. Nick Pugliese, "Nothing Bothers Emmitt," *The Sporting News* (November 13, 1987), p. 31.

11. Ibid.

12. Ibid.

Chapter 4

1. Paul Zimmerman, "The 100-Yard Dasher," *Sports Illustrated* (October 21, 1991), p. 74.

2. Steve Delsohn, *The Emmitt Zone* (New York: Crown Publishers, Inc., 1994), p. 104.

3. Ibid.

4. Paul Tagliabue, ESPN-TV telecast, April 1990.

5. Zimmerman, p. 74.

6. Leigh Montville, "A Man of Vision," *Sports Illustrated* (February 15, 1994), p. 148.

7. Tom Shatel, "Smith Off to a Running Start," *Dallas Morning News* (September 24, 1990), p. 16.

8. Zimmerman, p. 76.

Chapter 5

1. Dan Noxon, "Cowboys' Smith Shoulders the Load," *Dallas Morning News* (September 2, 1991), p. 18.

2. Rick Gosselin, "Cowboys Update—Aikman

Likes the View," *Dallas Morning News* (September 24, 1991), p. 5.

3. Jeff Rude, "Rushing Milestone for Smith, Win for Cowboys Coincide Again," *Dallas Morning News* (December 30, 1991), p. 9.

4. Rick Gosselin, "Lions End Cowboys' Season, 38–6," *Dallas Morning News* (January 6, 1992), p. 1.

Chapter 6

1. Tim Cowlishaw, "Dallas Decks Redskins, 23–10," *Dallas Morning News* (September 8, 1992), p. 1.

2. Ed Werder, "Smith Finds Holes in Raiders' Defense," *Dallas Morning News* (October 26, 1992), p. 8.

3. Tim Cowlishaw, "Victory Sets Cowboys Apart," *Dallas Morning News* (November 2, 1992), p. 1.

4. Tim Cowlishaw, "A Cinch Clincher—Dallas Captures NFC East With 41–17 Rout of Atlanta," *Dallas Morning News* (December 22, 1992), p. 1.

5. Scott Ostler, "Cowboys Concerned About Field Conditions," *San Francisco Chronicle* (January 11, 1993), p. 1.

Chapter 7

1. Leigh Montville, "A Man of Vision," *Sports Illustrated* (February 15, 1994), p. 142.

2. Paul Zimmerman, "One-Man Gang," *Sports Illustrated* (January 10, 1994), p. 36.

3. Don Norcross, "Johnson Sticks to Guns," *San Diego Union-Tribune* (January 22, 1994), p. 1.

4. Peter King, "Dare To Be Great," *Sports Illustrated* (January 24, 1994), p. 22.

Chapter 8

1. Mike Fisher, "Smith Plans Surgery, Talks of Team Trouble," *Fort Worth Star-Telegram* (February 23, 1994), p. 1.

2. Jim Reeves, "For Love or Glory," *Fort Worth Star-Telegram* (July 24, 1994), p. 1.

3. John Madden, FOX-TV telecast, September 4, 1994.

4. Wayne Lockwood, "Oh, the Pain," *San Diego Union-Tribune* (January 16, 1995), p. 7.

5. Ed Werder, "Emmitt Smith Has Done It All, But He Says That's Not Enough," *Dallas Morning News* (September 1, 1994), p. 1.

6. Leigh Montville, "A Man of Vision," *Sports Illustrated* (February 15, 1994), p. 151.

7. Peter King, "Dare To Be Great," *Sports Illustrated* (January 24, 1994), p. 24.

Career Statistics

YEAR	TEAM	G	RUSHING					RECEIVING		
			ATT	YDS	AVG	TD	REC	YDS	TD
1987	Gators	11	229	1,341	5.8	13	25	184	0
1988	Gators	8	187	988	5.3	9	10	72	0
1989	Gators	11	284	1,599	5.6	14	21	207	1
College Totals		30	700	3,928	5.6	36	56	463	1
1990	Cowboys	16	241	937	3.9	11	24	228	0
1991	Cowboys	16	365	1,593	4.3	12	49	258	1
1992	Cowboys	16	373	1,713	4.6	18	59	335	1
1993	Cowboys	14	283	1,486	5.3	9	57	414	1
1994	Cowboys	15	368	1,484	4.0	21	50	341	1
1995	Cowboys	16	377	1,773	4.7	25	62	375	0
NFL Totals		93	2,007	8,986	4.5	96	301	1,951	4

Where to Write Emmitt Smith

Mr. Emmitt Smith
c/o Dallas Cowboys
One Cowboys Parkway
Irving, TX 75063

Index